Contents

Words in **bold** are in the glossary on page 28.

All about me

My name is Leonel and I am seven years old. I live in a city called Peterborough, which is in the **county** of Cambridgeshire in England. I like watching motor racing on TV. I also enjoy playing football and riding my bike.

Sometimes I cycle to school with my cousin Mauro.

My family comes from Portugal. We moved to Britain two years ago. At school, I speak **English** with my friends, and at home, I speak **Portuguese** with my family.

Meeting people

What is your name?
Como se chama?

My name is
O meu nome é...

Hi	*Olá*
Thank you	*Obrigado*
Goodbye	*Adeus*

Look out for more Portuguese words in this book!

When I go out with my mum, we speak Portuguese together.

Meet my family

At mealtimes, my family likes to talk a lot!

I live with my mum, my brother Igor and my sisters Natacha, Tatiana and Margarida. I am the youngest in our house. My mum has three sisters and two brothers, who are my aunts and uncles. They all live in Peterborough too.

This photo of me and my brother and sisters was taken before we moved to Britain. Now, Natacha is 11, Igor is 12, Tatiana is 13 and Margarida is 15.

Some of my family still live in Portugal. My dad lives there with my baby brother Leo. My grandma also lives in Portugal. She doesn't want to move to Britain, even though she misses her children and grandchildren.

Family words

These are Portuguese words for people in your family.

Mum	*Mãe*
Dad	*Pai*
Sister	*Irmã*
Brother	*Irmão*
Grandma	*Avó*
Grandad	*Avô*

My dad

My grandma

My dad and grandma live a long way away, but I can talk to them on the phone.

About Portugal

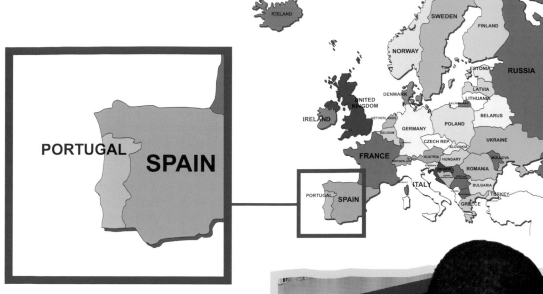

Portugal is a country in Western **Europe**. It is about the same size as Scotland. It takes two and a half hours to fly from London, the **capital city** of Britain, to Lisbon, the capital city of Portugal.

Sometimes I look for Portugal on a map. It is next to Spain.

When we lived in Portugal, we loved going to the beach. This is me and my family at the seaside, about 50 km north of Lisbon.

There are mountains in the north of Portugal. Spain is to the east, and the **Atlantic Ocean** is to the west. About two thirds of people in Portugal live near the **coast**. The **climate** is very warm and dry in the south of the country.

Leonel's mum says:

"Leonel really liked swimming when we lived in Portugal. It is always so hot there in the summer."

My life in Portugal

I was born in Lisbon, which is a big city.
It is much bigger than Peterborough.

Lisbon is in southwest Portugal. It is a city by the sea.

PORTUGAL

LISBON

Many tourists visit Lisbon every year. It is a very old, beautiful city.

Many shops and restaurants in Portuguese cities stay open until late at night, and families often go out together in the evening.

My family lived in an **apartment** in Lisbon. I used to think our apartment block looked like a hotel!

In Portuguese cities, many people live in apartments.

When I was little, my big sister Margarida looked after me at home when our mum was busy.

Leonel's mum says:

"Leonel loves his sister Margarida. When Leonel was a baby, her name was the first thing he learnt to say."

This is me when I was two years old, and this is my oldest sister, Margarida.

Moving to Britain

We travelled to Britain by plane. I was happy on the journey, because I like flying.

My family moved to Britain when I was five years old. We moved so that my mum could find work in this country. It was hard for my mum to leave her friends and family behind in Portugal. She still misses Portugal quite a lot.

Leonel's mum says:

"In Lisbon, it is easy to meet friends and go out in the evening. Peterborough is much quieter, and this is hard for me to get used to."

Peterborough

We came to live in Peterborough. At first, we stayed with my aunt and cousins, but then we moved into our own home. Our new house is bigger than the apartment we had in Lisbon.

I brought my fish and dog with me to Britain. I cuddle them every night.

My new hometown

We live in Dogsthorpe, which is in northeast Peterborough, about 2 km from the city centre. There are some good parks and places to play in Dogsthorpe. I like playing on the climbing frames at the park near my school.

My favourite superhero is Spiderman, and I love climbing.

I enjoy cooking, and can make pizza and pancakes, and also tasty cakes and biscuits. Sometimes I go shopping with my mum to buy things to cook. We usually go to the supermarket, but sometimes we go to the local shops.

In Peterborough, most of the shops are much smaller than in Lisbon.

Leonel's mum says:

"Leonel got used to living in Britain very quickly. I think this is because he hadn't lived in Portugal for long before he moved here."

Going to school

In Portugal, children start school when they are six. I was too young to go to school in Lisbon. When we moved to Peterborough, I started at Dogsthorpe Infant school. I was there for two years, then I moved up to the Junior school.

Dogsthorpe Junior School is next door to my old infant school.

Mrs Arya is the **language** teacher at my new junior school. She helps me to improve my English.

It was hard for me when I started school in Britain, because I couldn't speak any English and I didn't understand what people were saying. My teachers were kind to me, and I began to learn the language. It is much easier now, because I can understand and say more.

Miss Hawkey, Leonel's teacher, says:

"Leonel settled quickly into Year 3 and is happy in my class. He is quite good at speaking English, but he still finds reading and writing difficult."

My school day

My school day begins at 8.45am and ends at 3.15pm. In the mornings, I usually walk to school with my mum. My favourite lesson is maths, which I do every day.

My teacher this year is called Miss Hawkey. She helps me understand maths problems.

Leonel's mum says:

"In Portugal, the school day is longer than in Britain. Children there start school at 8am, and some older children don't finish until 6pm."

I eat a packed lunch at lunchtime, and then I go outside into the playground to play with my friends. My best friends are called Lewis, Samir, Jaegar and Ronan. We all love football!

When I am with my friends, we speak in English together.

My free time

Mauro is nine years old. He goes to the same school as me.

At the weekend, I like to play with my cousin Mauro. We go to the park on our bikes, and sometimes we go to the children's play centre near my house. We also enjoy playing computer games at home.

Leonel's cousin Mauro says:

"It's fun cycling with Leonel. We both like doing big jumps on our bikes when we go to the park."

Sometimes I go with Mum to Dogsthorpe library, to look at books. The library is close to my school, so it is easy to get to. I find reading difficult, but I practise as much as I can, to get better at it.

I can read in English, but I haven't learned to read in Portuguese yet.

Keeping traditions

We are **Catholics**, so Christmas is an important **festival** for us.

My family keep some Portuguese **traditions**. Late at night on Christmas Eve, we eat **'bacalhau'**. This is a special dinner of salted codfish with vegetables. After midnight, we give each other presents, dressed in our best pyjamas.

New Year's Eve is a time for parties, with music and lots of dancing.

At midnight on New Year's Eve, we eat a single grape each time the clock chimes. The 12 grapes we eat are meant to bring health and happiness for every month of the New Year.

Some special greetings

Here are some Portuguese greetings for special days of the year.

Merry Christmas	*Feliz Natal*
Happy New Year	*Feliz Ano Novo*
Happy Easter	*Feliz Páscoa*
Happy Birthday	*Feliz Aniversário*

My future

My school friends have helped me to learn how to speak English.

When I first came to Britain, I was excited about making new friends. I hope I will always make lots of friends in my life, because this makes me feel happy.

Miss Hawkey, Leonel's teacher, says:

"Leonel has made good friends at school and his English is getting better all the time. If he has a problem with something, the other children will always help him out."

When I grow up, I want to help people in the job that I do. Maybe I will become a doctor one day. I would really like to work with babies and children in a hospital.

My teachers at school are pleased with me, because I try to work hard.

Glossary

apartment
A flat, or set of rooms, where some people live.

Atlantic Ocean
The large sea between the continents of Europe and North America.

bacalhau
A traditional Portuguese dish of salted codfish and vegetables, which is served at the Christmas Eve supper.

capital city
The most important city in a country.

Catholic
Belonging to the Catholic faith. Roman Catholics are Christians that are led by the Pope in Rome.

climate
The usual pattern of weather in a place.

coast
The seashore, and the land that is near the sea.

county
One of the large areas that Britain is divided into.

English
The name for the main language that is spoken in Britain, and some other countries around the world.

Europe
One of the seven continents – large areas of land – of the world.

festival
A time of special, sometimes religious celebration.

hometown
The town where you live.

language
The words used by a group of people to communicate with each other.

Portuguese
The name for the language that is spoken in Portugal, Brazil and some African countries.

tradition
A belief, custom or habit that has not changed for a very long time.

Portugal fact file

- Lisbon is the capital city of Portugal. The distance between Lisbon and London is 1,402 km.

- The population of Portugal is about 10.5 million. Over two million people live in the capital city, Lisbon.

- In Portugal, people use the Euro currency. This is also used in many other European countries. One hundred cents make up one Euro.

- Fishing is an important industry in Portugal. Many traditional Portuguese dishes are made with fish, for example clam soup and cod fishcakes.

- Cycling and football are very popular in Portugal. José Azevedo is a famous Portuguese cyclist, and Cristiano Ronaldo is an international football star.

- Most people in Portugal are Roman Catholics. There are some Protestant Christians, and a small number of Muslims, Jews, Buddhists and Hindus.

- Every year, about six weeks before Easter, carnivals happen all over Portugal to mark Mardi Gras (Shrove Tuesday, or the beginning of Lent).

- Portuguese children start primary school when they are six years old, and go to secondary school when they are 12. They can leave school at 15, but many stay on until they are 18.

Portuguese flag

Index

Further information

Websites

www.visitportugal.com
www.portugal.org
www.PortugalLife.co.uk
www.cyberschoolbus.un.org
(Click on 'Country at a Glance' and select Portugal)
These websites give general information about Portugal.

www.visitlisboa.com
This website gives information about Lisbon, the city where Leonel and his family used to live.

Note to parents and teachers: Please note that these websites are **not** specifically for children and we strongly advise that Internet access is supervised by a responsible adult.